Welcome to Southsea

Southsea Castle was built on the orders of King He[nry]
and was an active military base for over 400 years. Toda[y]
in its role as a lively museum and historic [site].

During the castle's long and chequered history it was often badly neglected; but its key position defending the approaches to Portsmouth harbour ensured that whenever foreign danger threatened it had to be updated to meet the demands of new developments in artillery and fortifications.

Southsea Castle is now owned by Portsmouth City Council, and run by the City Museums and Records Service. We hope this guide will enhance your enjoyment of its fascinating past and the many exciting things you can experience at the castle today.

A Bird's-eye View

This auxiliary battery dates from *c*.1850. Access to it is via the counterscarp gallery.

A brick tunnel, known as a counterscarp gallery, was built round the outer side of the moat in 1813–14, with loopholes to enable the garrison to fire into the moat.

This grassy bank gives an idea of the sloping earthwork, or glacis, added on three sides of the castle in the late 17th century, to shield its vulnerable walls from enemy guns.

The lighthouse was built at the request of the Admiralty in the 1820s to assist navigation into Portsmouth harbour. It still operates today, with an automatic light.

The caponier was a tunnel linking the castle with the counterscarp gallery. It has a sloping roof to deflect enemy shells.

In the late 17th century a substantial platform for 30 guns was constructed where the promenade is today. It was undermined by the sea and what remained was used as a breakwater in 1813–14.

The south bastion was originally a pointed or 'angled' bastion, but was given a rounded form in 1813–14. The level was raised in 1850 so that the guns would overlook the flanks of the castle. The top of the parapet was built up using brick. This was thought to be less likely to splinter than stone if hit by an enemy missile.

Between the wars motor transport sheds were built in the castle complex. The last of these was incorporated into the D-Day Museum.

The east and west auxiliary batteries were built in the 1860s to increase the castle's fire-power. They were landscaped in the 1960s.

What remains of the red-brick 'gorge' wall, built in the 1860s to enclose the site, can be seen along the northern side of the car park.

The north bastion was reconstructed by Major-General Fisher in 1813–14, some 9 metres (30 feet) to the north of the original angled bastion, to make space for barrack rooms with a gun platform above.

The east and west gun platforms were the main batteries of Henry VIII's castle, and were originally solid. The barrack rooms below were created in 1813–14, and now contain historical displays.

The courtyard on three sides of the keep is called the bailey. A variety of guns are on display round the bailey.

The moat was always a dry one, but it was an important line of defence.

The keep was part of Henry VIII's original castle. It now houses the castle's displays on the military history of Portsmouth.

The curtain wall, or outer wall of the castle, was faced with Purbeck stone in 1813–14, so the Tudor section cannot now be distinguished from that of the Napoleonic period.

The Castle Today & Yesterday

THE ENTRANCE
Over the entrance to the castle is a stone plaque bearing the royal coat of arms of King Charles II. In the 18th century it is recorded that there were two inscriptions at the castle which referred to the king and to the year 1683. Charles II came to Portsmouth in that year, so it is likely that among the places he visited was Southsea Castle to inspect the improvements made by his chief military engineer, Sir Bernard de Gomme. When the north curtain wall was moved in 1813–14 the royal coat of arms was put back over the new entrance.

The bridge across the dry moat originally had a hinged section which fitted into a rectangular recess round the entrance. The slots and pulleys for the chains can still be seen, as can part of the winding gear.

THE RAMPARTS
From the bailey four staircases lead up to the gun platforms. These are made of granite blocks, sloping down towards the parapet in order to absorb the recoil of the guns. The bastion facing inland, created in 1813–14, is armed with 32-pounder smooth-bore, muzzle-loading guns, the typical armament of the Napoleonic period. The seven positions for guns on traversing platforms overlooking the sea were constructed in 1850.

ABOVE:
King Charles II's coat of arms over the castle entrance. During his reign, major improvements were made to the castle by Sir Bernard de Gomme.

RIGHT:
A section of the counterscarp gallery running round the outer wall of the moat. It is linked to the bailey by a tunnel known as the caponier.

ABOVE:
A 64-pounder (71cwt) rifled muzzle-loader. The barrel was made at the Royal Gun Factory, Woolwich in 1872.

ABOVE:
The lighthouse at Southsea Castle was built in the 1820s. The lighthouse keeper and his family lived in two rooms on the left of the castle entrance.

THE KEEP

The most prominent feature of the castle is the square keep. Its walls, made of rough stone bonded with natural clay, are up to 3 metres (10 feet) thick. Much of the exterior is the original Tudor stonework, though many alterations and repairs have been made over the centuries.

The bars on the windows are a relic of the period when the castle was used as a military prison (1844–50). By tradition, the two recesses covered by slates in the stonework above the entrance to the keep held a gallows.

The red-brick interior of the keep and the spiral staircase onto the roof date from the extensive reconstruction undertaken by Fisher in 1813–14 to increase accommodation at the castle. The ceilings were vaulted to strengthen them against enemy shells descending from above, and also to support the weight of the guns on the roof. The four gun positions on the roof were supplied with ammunition by hoists running up through channels which can be seen in the ceiling.

The Lighthouse

Harry Whitman, pictured here with his wife Bessie, son Billy and four-year-old daughter Molly, took up the post of lighthouse keeper at the beginning of 1912. Not long after this photograph was taken tragedy struck. In March 1913 Molly caught diphtheria and scarlet fever and died. The rooms at the castle were condemned by public health officials, and the family moved out. Harry continued to serve as lighthouse keeper until his retirement in 1927, and never had a day's illness or missed a night at his lamp.

The top of the keep gives an excellent view of the Solent and the sea forts constructed in the 1860s.

On the seaward side of the keep are three magazines, constructed in 1813–14. Behind the magazines is a passageway leading to the caponier, which provides access to the counterscarp gallery. The caponier gave rise in later years to the legend that the castle is linked to Spitbank fort by a secret passageway beneath the seabed.

THE BAILEY

Facing onto the bailey are barrack rooms, built of brick by Major-General Fisher in 1813–14. Like the interior of the keep, the rooms have vaulted ceilings to strengthen them. The line of the Tudor north curtain wall, demolished by Fisher, was uncovered during restoration work and is indicated in the bailey next to the Tudor well, which was excavated at the same time. Artefacts recovered from the well, including stone cannon balls, are on display in the keep.

The Tudor well became redundant when Fisher created a new reservoir under the western bailey. Its extent is shown by the paved area that we see today. The pump against the keep wall was used to pump water up from the reservoir.

The Building of Southsea Castle

'Your Highness's new fortress here ... may be called a castle, both for the compass, strength and beauty – and the device and fashion thereof is strange and marvellously praised of all men that have seen it.
I dare say your Majesty had never so great a piece of work done and so substantial, in so little time, as all skilful men that have seen it do report.'

SIR ANTHONY KNYVET TO KING HENRY VIII, 22 OCTOBER 1544

Construction began in spring 1544, prompted by Henry VIII's fears of a French attack on Portsmouth. Work proceeded as fast as possible on the new castle, positioned to command the deep-water channel into Portsmouth at the point where it brought ships closest to the shore.

The rapid progress was set out in reports to the king made by Sir Anthony Knyvet. As Governor of Portsmouth he supervised the work, together with John Chaderton, captain of the Portsmouth garrison. On 10 June 1544 Knyvet reported that ten days' bad weather had hindered the arrival of building supplies from the Isle of Wight; nevertheless the keep was up to the first floor and the seaward wall was nearly 2 metres (6 feet) high. A week later he wrote that the castle would be far enough advanced to mount guns within 12 days, but he complained that so far only two small brass 'sacres', which fired a 6-pound shot, had arrived.

On 8 July Sir Anthony wrote somewhat anxiously that he understood the king had been told that the castle was already fully defensible – 'the which is not'. The keep was up to the second floor and the seaward wall to the parapet, but the defences on the land side were not so advanced. Only a small quantity of gunpowder and the two sacres had been delivered, along with a 'good store of bows, arrows, bills and pikes'.

ABOVE RIGHT:
The Tudor re-enactment group Bills & Bows on parade at Southsea Castle.

LEFT:
The Mary Rose *is shown sinking as Henry VIII rides towards Southsea Castle on 19 July 1545. The original Tudor wall painting of the scene was lost when Cowdray House in Sussex was destroyed by fire in 1793. Fortunately an engraving had been published earlier, thus preserving this view.*

By mid-August the keep was at roof level, in spite of a continuing shortage of funds to pay the workforce. Throughout the summer Sir Anthony repeatedly urged that further money be sent, yet lack of it meant that workmen often left or had to be discharged. Nevertheless, by October, at least £3,000 had been spent in six months of construction work. Of this sum, £1,300 is known to have come from the proceeds of the Dissolution of the Monasteries.

Sir Anthony Knyvet appointed John Chaderton as chief captain of the new castle, 'with custody and profit of the marshes and moors adjoining it'. Chaderton was given charge of all the guns that had been sent – 'too little for half the place', as Knyvet complained to the king. There were 12 gunners, 8 soldiers and a porter, according to Knyvet the fewest considering the greatness of the place. Yet on 8 October, he wrote proudly to Lord Wriothesley, the High Chancellor, that such a fortress had never been built at so little cost, and that he hoped the king would be pleased with the castle, 'which was of his Majesty's own device' – that is to say, Henry VIII himself had been responsible for the castle's design.

ABOVE:
Finds from the well included stone cannon balls and holed flint pebbles that were used as counter-weights for the bucket.

RIGHT:
The Tudor well in the bailey against the north-east wall. It was later filled in, but was then re-excavated in the 1965 restoration.

7

His Majesty's Own Device

Southsea Castle was one in a series of forts built by Henry VIII, the most ambitious scheme of coastal defence since Roman times. The programme began in 1539 when the king's conflict with the Pope over his divorce led to a short-lived alliance between Francis I of France and Emperor Charles V of Spain, and a combined invasion of England looked a very real possibility.

The first of these forts to be built looked very different from Southsea Castle which, even allowing for flattery on Sir Anthony Knyvet's part, the king certainly played a part in designing. Forts such as St Mawes in Cornwall and Deal in Kent had large rounded bastions clustered about a circular keep.

Henry VIII had a great interest in the science of fortifications and artillery. His campaign in France, which culminated in the capture of Boulogne in September 1544, would have given him the opportunity to study new continental ideas on fortress design. These had their origins in Italy where rounded towers and bastions had been replaced by straight walls, meeting to form pointed, or angled, bastions. These presented the minimum target to enemy guns, whilst the defenders could fire right along the length of the walls of an angled bastion, leaving no 'dead ground' where attacking troops could shelter.

Under the influence of Italian ideas, and probably also the need for ease and speed of construction, Southsea Castle was built with a square keep, rectangular gun platforms to the east and west, and, most significantly, angled bastions on the north and south sides. It

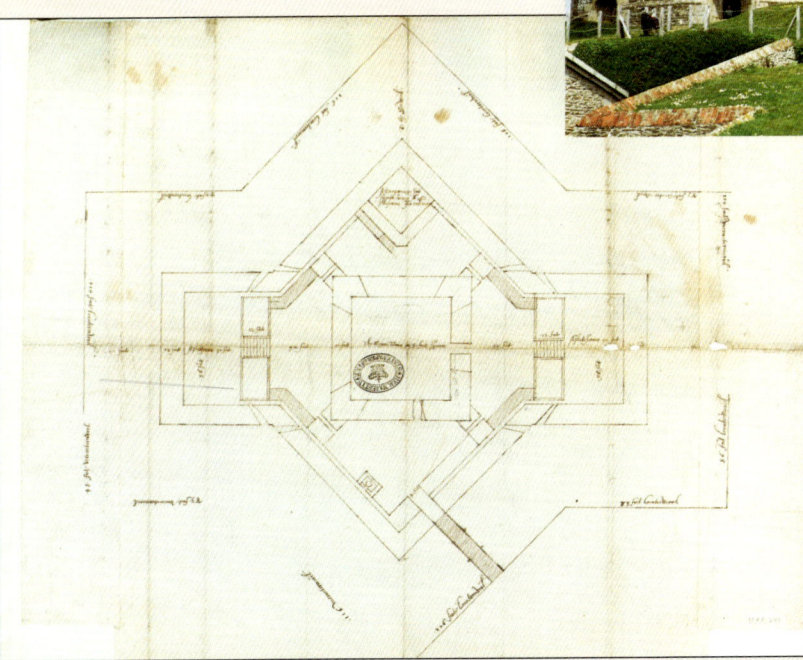

LEFT:
The earliest known plan of Southsea Castle, dated 1577. It shows the progress of work on enlarging the moat. No additional work seems to have been done at the time of the Armada (1588), though we can assume that the castle was in a high state of readiness.

8

ABOVE:
Henry VIII and his court visit Southsea Castle, courtesy of Bills & Bows.

LEFT:
St Mawes Castle near Falmouth shows the characteristic rounded bastions of Henry VIII's first artillery forts, in contrast to the angular design of Southsea Castle. The rounded form was based on principles which originated in northern Europe, particularly Germany, and also followed in the tradition of late medieval British castles.

RIGHT:
In this tableau an early breech-loading gun has exploded as the Mary Rose *sinks on 19 July 1545. The tableau is set by one of the keep's Tudor gunports. At some time it had been blocked up, but it was re-opened during the castle's restoration in the 1960s.*

therefore represents a break with the past, and is a landmark in the development of fortifications in England.

The new design looked as if it was about to be put to the test when, on 18 July 1545, the French fleet rounded the Isle of Wight and entered the Solent. The following day the *Mary Rose* went down with nearly 700 men on board, witnessed by Henry himself. The French put light forces ashore on the Isle of Wight for a short time, but did not risk any more whilst the English fleet was still threatening them. While in Portsmouth, the king no doubt inspected Southsea Castle closely. Alarmed about its ability to withstand a sudden assault, he ordered a number of modifications.

Eight 'flankers' were created, openings for guns near the foot of the curtain wall, to fire at enemy soldiers scaling the walls from the dry moat. Within the bailey, hollow walls or 'traverses' were built from the corners of the keep to the curtain wall, dividing the courtyard into four compartments. Defenders could open fire through loopholes from within the traverses. Guardhouses were built on either side of the steps to the east and west platforms, to control access to these all-important gun batteries from inside the bailey.

By the end of Henry's reign in 1547, Southsea Castle, heavily armed with a total of 17 guns, was a formidable fortress.

The Castle under the Stuarts

LEFT:
This drawing from c.1670 shows what Southsea Castle must have looked like at the time of the Civil War.

RIGHT:
The Civil War brought to life at the castle by the re-enactment group Captayne Henry Hazzard's Company.

During the early 17th century, the castle was very much neglected. A Privy Council report of 1623 declared that it was 'verie ill prepared for defence in any occasion that might befall both through the defect of men and munition'. Worse was to come. In 1627 the keep was gutted by a fire that started in one of the chimneys.

Despite appeals by the commander of the castle, eight years passed before King Charles I gave orders that 210 loads of New Forest timber should be sent for the repair of the living quarters. Although overdue, the work was done well: 'It hath dainty chambers in it, fit to entertain a prince.'

The year 1642 saw the outbreak of the Civil War between the King and Parliament. The Governor of Portsmouth, Colonel Goring, declared his support for Charles I. Local Parliamentary forces under Colonel Norton of Southwick besieged the town, and resolved to capture Southsea Castle. Its military strength was problematic. It boasted 14 guns and various small arms – but a garrison of only 12 men! Nevertheless, two troops of Parliamentary cavalry and 400 infantry assembled for the assault one Saturday night in September. All the castle's guns had been moved to face inland, but some of the attackers got between the castle and the sea. In readiness, a few jumped the 5 metres (16 feet) down into the moat.

At the entrance, a Parliamentarian trumpeter sounded a parley. The commander of the castle, Captain Chaloner, had been appointed to the post in 1640, 'with all fees and profits, during good behaviour'; but his behaviour now left much to be desired. He had spent Saturday drinking with Colonel Goring in Portsmouth. Even his own men reported that he had 'more drink in his head than was befitting such a time and service'. Now, roused from an intoxicated sleep by the summons to surrender, he asked if the attackers could 'stay until morning and he would consider it'.

At that, 80 Parliamentarian soldiers scaled the walls. Heavily outnumbered, the garrison had no choice but to surrender. According to one source, Chaloner then 'fell to drinking of the King and Parliament's health in sack with our officers'. At his suggestion, guns were fired towards the town as a signal that the castle had been taken. Colonel Goring responded with at least 30 shot so that everyone had to dive for cover.

The only casualties that night were some soldiers who hurt themselves jumping into the moat. For the first and only time in its history, Southsea Castle had seen action. With the castle and Gosport in enemy hands, Portsmouth itself surrendered within three days.

After the restoration of Charles II, maritime conflict with the Dutch meant that Portsmouth's security was again threatened. In 1665 the King initiated major improvements to the town's defences, masterminded by his Dutch-born chief military engineer, Sir Bernard de Gomme. To increase Southsea Castle's firepower, de Gomme built a substantial new platform between the castle and the sea, mounting 30 guns. For better defence, he constructed a large sloping earthwork, or glacis, on the landward side to shield the walls from attacking artillery. This gave the castle a new lease of life, though in 1690 a lady traveller, Celia Fiennes, wrote that it looked 'very fine, but I think it is but of little strength and service'.

BELOW:
A plan of 'Zouthzea Castele' dating from around 1668 showing proposed additions of a protective glacis and new platform for guns on the seaward side.

LEFT:
The morning after the storming of Southsea Castle – an artist's impression of the scene at dawn as a still inebriated Captain Chaloner is led away.

Picturesque Decay

During the 18th century Southsea Castle became increasingly dilapidated and outmoded as a fortress. Disaster struck in 1759 when a great explosion shattered the castle. The 72nd Regiment of Foot, commanded by the Duke of Richmond, was camped on Southsea Common. The soldiers had permission to store their gunpowder and ball for muskets in a ground floor room on the eastern side of the castle. The day before the accident they had filled nine barrels with cartridges for their exercises. Above the storeroom were living quarters where women were preparing food. The floor was very old and it is thought that sparks from a large cooking fire fell through crevices onto some loose powder beneath. In the terrible explosion that followed 17 men, women and children were killed. There were some lucky escapes. One soldier of the 41st Invalid Regiment was blown right out of the castle but received only a bruised head. Another man, standing close to the explosion, was rendered unconscious but otherwise unhurt. When he was shaken, he 'awakened as out of a sleep, without any recollection of what had happened'. The east wing was extensively damaged; on the western side the force of the blast burst open a large magazine, but luckily did not ignite the contents.

In the 1770s the castle was described as being 'in a most shameful ruin'. In the 1780s, the Duke of Richmond, now Master-General of the Ordnance, ordered the demolition of the old Fort Cumberland at nearby Langstone Harbour so that a new 'star fort' could be built. Similarly, he reported in 1785 that Southsea Castle was 'of too bad a form to deserve the expense necessary to repair it. A square redoubt of a modern construction more advantageously and securely placed, a little further from the sea is proposed to be built in its stead.'

RIGHT:
A 1765 engraving. In 1785 the government purchased Southsea Common to prevent any building which would obstruct the field of fire between the castle and the town of Portsmouth a mile distant.

ABOVE:
A watercolour of the 1760s. A contemporary description refers to the castle's 'very strong battery of guns', but then goes on to say that 'in times of danger there is, or should be, a Governor and a competent number of soldiers; but for many years past it has been kept by an old sergeant and three or four men who sell cakes and ale.'

RIGHT:
Prelude to the explosion of August 1759 – a scene from the castle's Time Tunnel.

But nothing was done by the time war broke out with France in 1793. By early 1797 invasion was feared and urgent orders were sent to put the castle into a state of readiness; furnaces were built in the courtyard to heat red hot shot, a useful weapon against wooden ships. Then Admiral Jervis's victory off Cape St Vincent in February lifted the threat.

It is doubtful whether the castle could have done much to hinder an enemy, since the sea had demolished most of de Gomme's grand battery. In 1798 the castle had only eight 32-pounder and five 6-pounder guns. It was recorded that the gun carriages were 'very much in want of repair, the iron work being so decayed as to be scarcely fit for service'.

New renovation proposals were made in 1804, but despite Napoleon's invasion preparations, nothing was done. The castle had escaped demolition, but it seemed fated to remain in a state of picturesque decay.

LEFT:
One fascinating exhibit is this bronze 24-pounder from the Royal George *which sank at Spithead in 1782, with the loss of 900 lives. The barrel was recovered in 1834 by the diver John Deane.*

The Castle Reformed

ABOVE: *The Worcestershire Regiment of Militia is shown parading near Southsea Castle on 14 October 1800 in this oil painting by Richard Livesay. Working parties of militiamen such as these were used to rebuild the castle in 1813–14.*

In 1812 Major-General Benjamin Fisher became commander of the Royal Engineers in Portsmouth. He was 60 and had served 42 years in the army. Early in 1813 it fell to him to begin the long-delayed 'reform' of Southsea Castle – at an estimated cost of £18,105.5s.5d.

Rumours abounded that the large supply of oak and beech landed on the shore spelled the end for Henry VIII's fortress and that Fisher intended to build a completely new fort. He did not. The main object was to create accommodation for some 200 men in time of war and, to this end, the General reconstructed the interior of the keep and built barrack rooms on the eastern and western sides of the bailey. His most drastic alteration was to demolish the curtain wall on the northern side, and rebuild it some 9 metres (30 feet) further north. This made space for extra rooms, and also created a substantial new platform for guns above them.

Convict labour had been used to rebuild Fort Cumberland, but at Southsea Castle Fisher preferred to employ a mixed workforce of civilians and soldiers. When it was proposed to contract out all building works to civilians, Fisher protested to his superiors that using troops saved a great deal of public money. He added that that was another important advantage using military labour, 'viz. keeping down the high wages of the workmen, and breaking up any combination amongst them'.

Although de Gomme's grand battery facing the sea was not rebuilt, Fisher did improve the castle's strength in a variety of ways. He squared off the top of the keep by removing the Tudor watch-tower, and created four positions for 24-pounder guns on the roof. The angled bastion facing the sea was rounded off to create a larger curved battery with magazines underneath; and a counterscarp gallery was built in the outer wall of the moat, linked to the castle by a bomb-proof tunnel known as a caponier.

The bulk of the work was done in 1813–14, though it was not finished until 1816. General Fisher did not live to see its completion. On 29 September 1814 he committed suicide. No clues are provided by contemporary documents to explain the manner of his death, 'under circumstances awful in the contemplation and severely afflicting to his family, to his friends and to society'. He was buried at the Royal Garrison Church in Portsmouth. At Southsea Castle he is remembered by the inscription over the entrance to the courtyard: 'REFORMED MDCCCXIV [1814], MAJOR GENERAL FISHER, COMMANDING ROYAL ENGINEERS.'

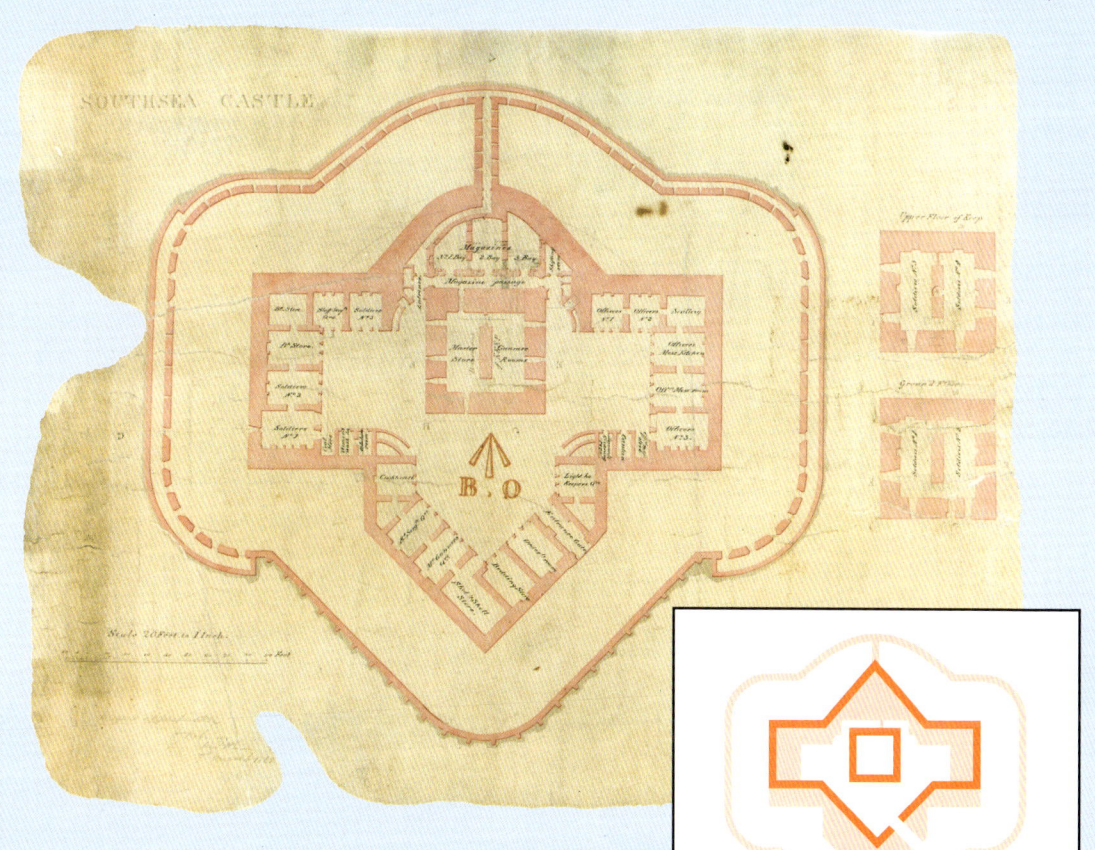

LEFT:
32-pounder guns of the type which would have been mounted on the landward side of the castle in 1814.

ABOVE:
An 1834 plan showing Fisher's arrangement of rooms and the counterscarp gallery.

■ Built by Henry VIII, 1544–45

■ Major-General Fisher's modifications, 1813–14

The Castle as a Prison

The castle was first used as a prison in the 17th century. In 1844 the barrack rooms built by Fisher were converted to house 150 military prisoners.
Since the castle, however, had to be 'always in all points ready for offence and defence', guns and stores were retained, and a sergeant from the Royal Artillery was appointed as both a warder and master gunner. To the relief of the respectable residents of Southsea, all the prisoners were moved to a new military prison at Forton in Gosport in 1850. The castle's time as a prison for soldiers is commemorated in the Time Tunnel of today, shown right.

The Castle Expands

In the mid-19th century a widespread fear of war with Napoleon III, combined with rapid changes in warship technology and the range and accuracy of guns, meant that Portsmouth's defences were constantly under scrutiny.

In 1850 Southsea Castle was strengthened by the addition of seven new 8-inch (65cwt) guns on the parapet looking out to sea. One critic, James Fergusson, was unimpressed. In his pamphlet *The Peril of Portsmouth* (1852), he declared that 'one broadside would probably finish the defences of Southsea Castle for ever'. By 1856 small auxiliary batteries had been built of earth on both sides of the castle, slightly detached from it, to provide emplacements for still more guns.

In 1860 a Royal Commission report led to the building of forts on Portsdown Hill. Long-range bombardment of the dockyard was the main concern, but the report also recommended that at the castle, 'which is in a most important position, raking the approach, additional batteries should be placed connecting the present auxiliary batteries with that work'. Construction of the east and west batteries began in 1863 and was completed by 1869. At the same time the whole complex, extending over 17 acres (6.8 ha), was enclosed on the land side by a high brick wall with loopholes to enable infantry to repel a raiding party attempting to overrun the batteries.

By 1886 the armament of the castle and its auxiliary batteries included 25 massive rifled muzzle-loading guns. A few years later these would all be redundant as Portsmouth's defences faced new challenges. By 1892 five 6-pounder QF ('quick-firing') guns had been mounted

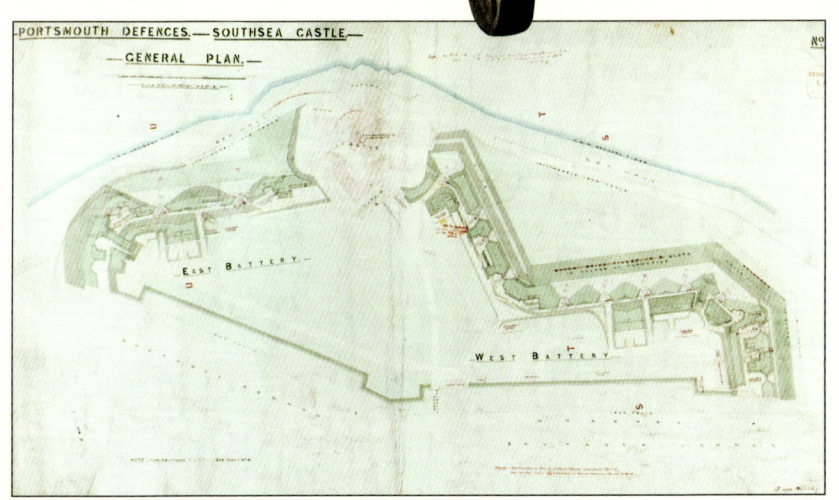

ABOVE:
The castle entrance is guarded by this Victorian muzzle-loading gun: an 1853 68-pounder.

LEFT:
An 1893 plan, showing the east and west batteries and the gorge wall of the 1860s.

LEFT:
A mock gun-boat attack on the castle formed part of the 1856 review to mark the end of the Crimean War. Well over half a million people came to see 254 ships inspected by Queen Victoria. The gun-boat attack was cut short when the Lieutenant-Governor of Portsmouth heard that he might have to pay for the ammunition!

attracted a large crowd, despite the bitter weather.' Work on the east battery was completed in August 1901, at a cost of £16,670.

In the lead up to the First World War, Southsea Castle was an important part of the 'Fortress Portsmouth' scheme, which encompassed the defence of Portsmouth and Southampton. In 1910 the east battery mounted two 9.2-inch BL and two 6-inch BL guns, whilst on the west battery there were three 12-pounder QF and one 4.7-inch QF guns. The old castle, now at the centre of a modern coastal defence complex, was used for the vital work of range and direction finding for the two main batteries.

at the castle to counter the threat from fast-moving torpedo boats. Three searchlights were installed to guard against a surprise night attack from the sea.

Furthermore, after a false start in the 1860s, BL (breech-loading) guns had proved themselves superior to muzzle-loaders. The 9.2-inch BL gun was chosen as the main coastal defence weapon, and was installed round Britain and throughout the Empire. Work on adapting the east battery at Southsea Castle for these and 6-inch BL guns began in 1899. In January 1900 *The Engineer* journal reported that the remaining unwanted muzzle-loaders were being slowly moved by hand across Southsea Common, which was 'an interesting sight and

As Southsea seafront became more popular, range practice sometimes had its problems as this 1892 cartoon shows.

COMBINED FIRING UNDER DIFFICULTIES

[Colonel trying in vain to clear the range]
"Bad cess to ye – I'm going to fire great big shott !!"

ABOVE:
A 9-inch rifled muzzle-loading gun on the west battery about 1890. The positions of the sea forts are marked on the granite plinth so that the gunners knew if the gun was pointing at one of them during practice firing.

17

The Two World Wars

When the First World War broke out in 1914, the castle's guns were manned by regular Royal Garrison Artillery and by No.4 (Portsmouth) Company of the Hampshire RGA Territorials. During 1915, however, men of No.4 Company were drafted abroad in growing numbers. In 1917 the guns were handed over to the 'citizen artillerists' of the newly formed Hampshire RGA Volunteers. The names of 27 members of No.4 Company killed in the war are recorded on a plaque in the Royal Garrison Church.

Despite many alerts, no German seaborne threat to Portsmouth materialized in either world war. After the fall of France in 1940, however, the castle was involved in a confrontation with a number of French naval vessels which had escaped to Spithead. On 23 June, at 8.10am, Southsea Castle received an urgent order: 'All guns to be manned and ready to open fire immediately. French ships are not to be allowed to leave.' One of the castle's 9.2-inch guns was trained on the ships, though this was only a bluff as it was not ready for action. A French destroyer, *Leopard*, returned the compliment by turning its guns towards the castle. The crisis passed, and on 2 July the French ships were taken over by boarding parties.

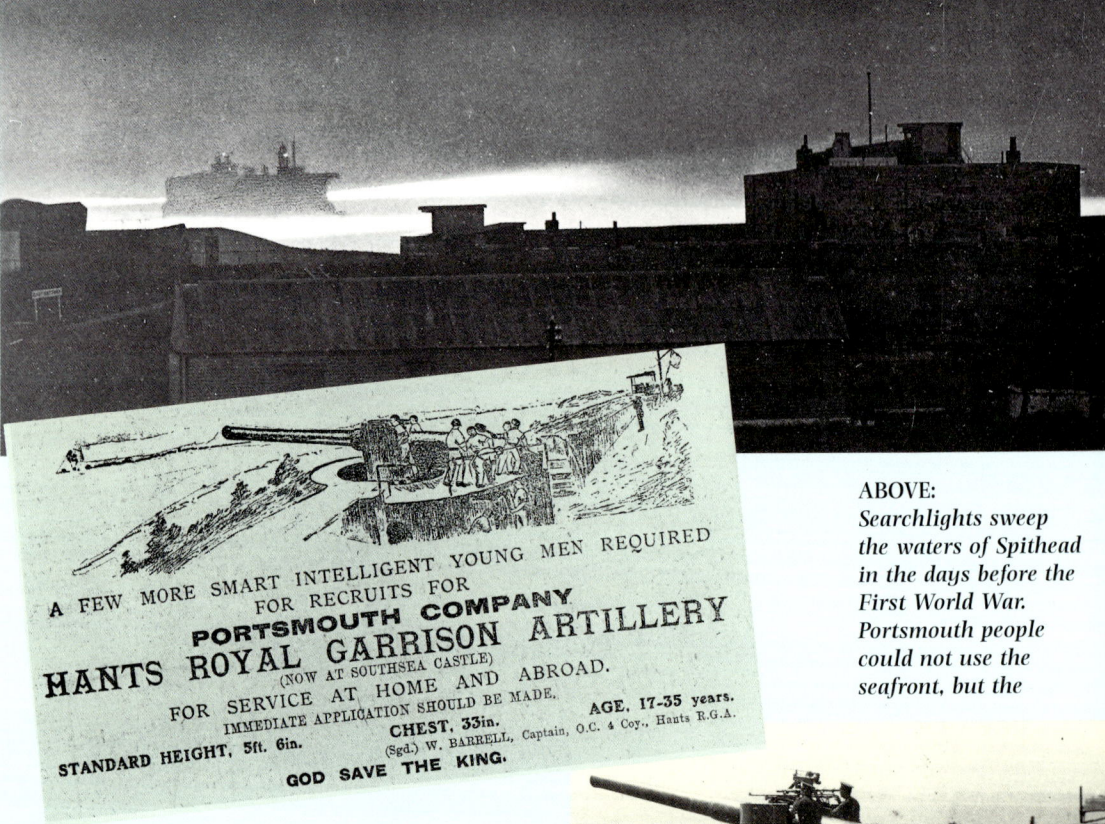

ABOVE:
Searchlights sweep the waters of Spithead in the days before the First World War. Portsmouth people could not use the seafront, but the

ABOVE:
A 1915 advert from the Portsmouth Evening News. A member of the garrison wrote: 'We do not seem to be having much luck in coming to grips with the German Fleet here, so we are all anxious to try conclusions with their army. However, to make this possible we must get the Company up to sufficient strength to allow an effective garrison to be left here, so let us all do our best to get more recruits.'

RIGHT:
Two 6-inch breech-loading guns on the east battery, c.1900.

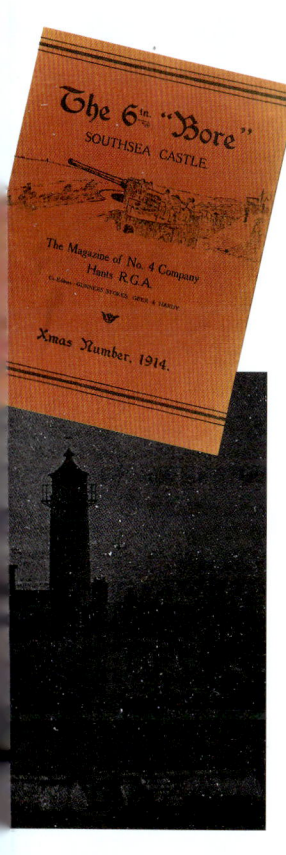

LEFT:
The castle garrison found time to produce a humorous house magazine.

In 1940 a young Lewis gunner at the castle, Bill Neal, found that the balloon barrage kept enemy planes out of range of his Lewis gun, but this was not necessarily a good thing: 'If you were busy on a gun you didn't notice what was going on and didn't have a chance to get frightened, but just having to sit there and watch – a front-line audience – was not so good.'

war 'brought its compensations in the daily processions of vessels of all kinds and the nightly display of searchlight wonders'.

ABOVE:
In 1941, Betty Prior of the ATS found herself billeted with nine other girls in the basement of the keep – 'in a dungeon! It was cold and wet and horrible ... The only things in the room were our beds and what is known as a barrack box with our belongings in, and a big, black stove and nothing else ... When we put the shovel into the bin for the coal the mice used to come out and we used to chase them with the shovel.'

It was from the air, rather than the sea, that the threat to Portsmouth came in the Second World War. German daylight raids began in July 1940. There had been a number of false alarms. 'We got a bit blasé about it in the end,' recalled Bill Neal, a young Lewis gunner stationed at the castle. 'It had come through that there were so many plus hostiles approaching. Never thought anything more about it until I looked up and saw what looked like a swarm of bees coming, and it was the actual Germans coming in this time and proceeding to drop stuff all over the place.' Southsea Castle was hit at least twice by incendiary bombs but the resulting fires were quickly extinguished.

Various units besides coast artillery were on duty at Southsea Castle during the war, and a bleak experience it could be. The Home Guard did nightly sentry duty, looking out to sea wrapped in blankets, whilst one Royal Engineer recalled a colleague nearly burning the keep down – in a repeat of 1627 – by using petrol to try to get a fire to light.

Gunner George Self, who manned old 3-inch naval guns on the East Battery, wrote that he was lucky not to have arrived until March 1940. Before that conditions had been 'so primitive that nearly all the gun station were ill (some seriously) during that first winter'. Yet in the end Gunner Self became quite attached to the castle. When his unit moved in 1941, he wrote regretfully: 'This place is quiet after Southsea with all its singing, chatter and general movement.' So perhaps the castle was not such a bad billet after all.

19

The Castle Restored

In 1956 the advent of missiles and airpower led to the abolition of coastal artillery in the army, and Southsea Castle became surplus to requirements. In 1960 Portsmouth City Council acquired the whole site for £35,000, the only conditions being that the council should preserve the castle in its proper setting; that a working lighthouse could be retained and that the Army would be able to fly a flag from the keep when required. Although the castle itself was in a sorry state, it was clear that it could become one of the most important and popular amenities on the front.

Portsmouth Council decided that the castle should be restored to its 19th-century appearance, and become a museum of the city's military heritage. This was accomplished by the council's architect's department (which subsequently won awards for the project), with the guidance of the local history curator, Bill Corney, who made Portsmouth's fortifications his lifetime's study. Work went ahead on removing the profusion of 20th-century structures on and around the castle, repairing the fabric and landscaping the surrounding area. In 1963 the foundations of the Tudor north curtain wall were discovered while drains were being dug in the bailey, and work was halted to allow archaeological investigation. The castle, with its new displays, was opened to the public in 1967.

BELOW:
When the castle was bought by Portsmouth City Council in 1960, much restoration was needed.

The stonemasons of Portsmouth City Council played an important part in the restoration of Southsea Castle – men such as Len Kidd, who spent more than eight years on the project. Len says, 'When you start a job it is often difficult to tear yourself away. You can't stop until you see how the thing has turned out. You get sentimental about the things you've done – there's part of me in Southsea Castle and it'll be there long after I'm gone.'

Today thousands of visitors every year explore Southsea Castle and enjoy the panoramic views of the Solent from its ramparts. The castle boasts fascinating displays, including the Time Tunnel, which takes visitors through a series of dramatic episodes in the castle's history. The castle is the home of the Fort Cumberland Guard, and regular events and historical re-enactments take place every year. The castle is also available as an unusual venue for private functions.

BELOW:
The Fort Cumberland Guard, the resident re-enactment group, have their own exhibition rooms at the castle.

RIGHT:
Southsea Castle today.

BELOW RIGHT:
Children's activities at the castle.

Acknowledgements

Written by Stephen Brooks.
Edited by John McIlwain.
Designed by Adrian Hodgkins Design.

All illustrations are © Portsmouth City Council (by Roger Skinner, Dave Wright, Sue Jackson, David Miller) except for:
The News, Portsmouth: p.18 inset, p.19 top right.
Imperial War Museum: p.17 right.
Public Records Office: p.8 bottom, p.15 top, p.16 bottom.
The Royal Collection © 1996 H.M. The Queen: front cover (Henry VIII).
The 64-pdr gun (p.4) and the 24-pdr gun (p.13) are by courtesy of Royal Armouries.

The artist's impression on p.10/11 is by Dave Russell.
The oral history interviewees were Alan Meaby, Bill Neal, Betty Prior and Vic Saul.
Typescript prepared by Greta Hicks and Liz Dunk.

Publication in this form © Pitkin Guides Ltd 1996.

No part of this publication may be reproduced by any means without the permission of Pitkin Guides Ltd and the copyright holders.

Printed in Great Britain.
ISBN 0 85372 809 7   196/15

For further information about Southsea Castle, please telephone 01705 827261

PITKIN
· GUIDES ·

AN EXTENSIVE SERIES ABOUT HISTORIC PLACES AND FAMOUS PEOPLE

•

Available by mail order
Free colour brochure and stock list available from:
Pitkin Guides, Healey House, Dene Road, Andover, Hampshire, SP10 2AA, UK.

Tel: 01264 334303 Fax: 01264 334110

ISBN 0-85372-809-7